D0403376

RISING TO THE CALL

RISING TO THE CALL

OS GUINNESS

W PUBLISHING GROUP™

www.wpublishinggroup.com

A Division of Thomas Nelson, Inc.
www.ThomasNelson.com

Published by W Publishing Group, a Division of Thomas Nelson, Inc., P.O. Box 141000, Nashville, Tennessee, 37214.

Unless otherwise indicated, Scripture quotations used in this book are from the Holy Bible, New International Version (NIV). Copyright © 1973, 1978, 1984, International Bible Society. Used by permission of Zondervan Bible Publishers.

Library of Congress Cataloging-in-Publication Data

Guinness, Os.
  Rising to the call / by Os Guinness.
    p. cm.
  ISBN 0-8499-1783-2
  1. Vocation—Christianity. 2. Spiritual life—Christianity. I. Title.
BV4740.G86 2003
248.4—dc21   2003000948

Printed in the United States of America

03 04 05 06 07 PHX 8 7 6 5 4 3 2 1

To
D.O.M.
and to C.J.
with love and gratitude

CONTENTS

INTRODUCTION

How do we each find and fulfill the central purpose of our lives? No theme I know strikes a deeper resonance with more people today than discovering life's purpose. It's a question, of course, but it's more—far, far more. It's a question that's a passion, a longing, a hunger, a restless stirring in our souls, a driving motivation that fires the deepest parts of our lives and taps into the most powerful sources of our energy.

This question, as we'll see, comes up at various points in life. This little book addresses many of them, but it is written for people at two moments in particular:

The first is the golden "big seven" years—the years between eighteen and twenty-five when childhood lies behind and you have climbed high enough to see the shimmering vistas ahead. But how do you choose when there is so much to choose from? And how do you choose well when you have more energy than experience and your excitement outstrips your wisdom? The notion of calling is the clearest, strongest guide to the challenges at that wonderful stage of life. There is no deeper meaning in life than to discover and live out your calling.

The second moment is a few years later: for those who realize they chose badly the first time—usually because they didn't know the notion of calling. They then wonder if they can have another chance, and how they can do a better job of choosing the second time around. Was novelist George Eliot right when she wrote, "It is never too late to be what you might have been"? The notion of calling is the deepest, surest encouragement at that particular moment in life. Your calling is deeper than your job, your career, and all your benchmarks of success. It is never too late to discover your calling.

So read this book and let your mind run deep—thinking over your life, your family, your gifts, your hopes, your dreams, your friends, your world, and your goals. No truth in all human history has changed more lives and changed more societies. It can change you. It can change the world through you. Or rather, *he* can—for there is no calling without a caller and down the centuries God's call has proved the ultimate Why in the human search for purpose. No one and nothing else even comes close.

—OS GUINNESS

1

THE ULTIMATE WHY

As you know, I have been very fortunate in my career and I've made a lot of money—far more than I ever dreamed of, far more than I could ever spend, far more than my family needs." The speaker was a prominent businessman at a conference near Oxford University. The strength of his determination and character showed in his face, but a moment's hesitation betrayed deeper emotions hidden behind the outward intensity. A single tear rolled slowly down his well-tanned cheek.

"To be honest, one of my motives for making so much money was simple—to have the money to hire people to do what I don't like doing. But there's one thing I've never been able to hire anyone to do for me: find my own sense of purpose and fulfillment. I'd give anything to discover that."

That issue—purpose and fulfillment—is one of the deepest issues in our modern world. At some point every one of us confronts the question: How do I find and fulfill the central purpose of my life? Other questions may come logically prior to and lie even deeper than this one—for example, Who am I? What is the meaning of life itself? But few questions are raised more loudly and more insistently today than the first. As modern people we are all on a search for significance. We desire to make a difference. We long to leave a legacy. We yearn, as Ralph Waldo Emerson put it, "to leave the world a bit better." Our passion is to know that we are fulfilling the purpose for which we are here on earth.

These passions can differ enormously—from an Olympic gold medal to a Hollywood Oscar to a Nobel Prize to an executive suite to the White House. Artists, scientists, and builders often labor to create a unique work that can live forever in their name. Politicians, business people, and administrators usually think of their monuments more in terms of institutions they have created and sustained. Parents, teachers, and counselors, by contrast, view their contribution in terms of lives shaped and matured. But for all the variety, the need for purpose is the same. As Thomas Carlyle wrote, "The man without a purpose is like a ship without a rudder—a waif, a nothing, a no-man."

All other standards of success—wealth, power, position, knowledge, friendships—grow tinny and hollow if we do not satisfy this deeper longing. For some people the hollowness leads to what Henry Thoreau described as "lives of quiet desperation"; for others the emptiness and aimlessness deepen into a stronger despair. In an early draft of Fyodor Dostoevsky's *The Brothers Karamazov,* the Inquisitor gives a terrifying account of what happens to the human soul when it doubts its purpose: "For the secret of man's being is not only to live . . . but to live for something definite. Without a firm notion of what he is living for, man will not accept life and will rather destroy himself than remain on earth. . . ."

Call it the greatest good (*summum bonum*), the ultimate end, the meaning of life, or whatever you choose. But finding and fulfilling the purpose of our lives comes up in myriad ways and in all the seasons of our lives:

Teenagers feel it as the world of freedom beyond home and secondary school beckons with a dizzying range of choices.

Graduate students confront it when the excitement of "the world is my oyster" is chilled by the thought that opening up one choice means closing down others.

Those in their early thirties know it when their daily work assumes its own brute reality beyond their earlier considerations of the wishes of their parents, the fashions of their peers, and the allure of salary and career prospects.

People in midlife face it when a mismatch between their gifts and their work reminds them daily that they are square pegs in round holes. Can they see themselves "doing that for the rest of their lives"?

Mothers feel it when their children grow up, and they wonder which high purpose will fill the void in the next stage of their lives.

People in their forties and fifties with enormous success suddenly come up against it when their accomplishments raise questions concerning the social responsibility of their success and, deeper still, the purpose of their lives.

People confront it in all the varying transitions of life—from moving homes to switching jobs to breakdowns in marriage to crises of health. Negotiating the changes feels longer and worse than the changes themselves because transition challenges our sense of personal meaning.

Those in their later years often face it again. What does life add up to? Were their successes real, and were they worth the trade-offs? Having gained a whole world, however huge or tiny, have we sold our souls cheaply and missed the point of it all? As Walker Percy wrote, "You can get all A's and still flunk life."

This issue, the question of his own life-purpose, is what drove the Danish thinker Sören Kierkegaard in the nineteenth century. As he realized well, personal purpose is not a matter of philosophy or theory. It is not purely objective, and it is not inherited like a legacy. Many a scientist has an encyclopedic knowledge of the world, many a philosopher can survey vast systems of thought, many a theologian can unpack the profundities of religion, and many a journalist can seemingly speak on any topic raised. But all that is theory and, without a sense of personal purpose, vanity.

Deep in our hearts, we all want to find and fulfill a purpose bigger than ourselves. Only such a larger purpose can inspire us to heights we know we could never reach on our own. For each of us the real purpose is personal and passionate: to know what we are here to do, and why. Kierkegaard wrote in his *Journal*: "The thing is to understand myself, to see what God really wants me to do; the thing is to find a truth which is true *for me,* to find the *idea for which I can live and die.*"

TOO MUCH TO LIVE WITH,
TOO LITTLE TO LIVE FOR

In our day, this question is urgent for many, and there is a simple reason why. Three factors have converged to fuel a search for significance without precedent in human history. First, the search for the purpose of life is one of the deepest issues of our experiences as human beings. Second, the expectation that we can all live purposeful lives has been given a gigantic boost by modern society's offer of the maximum opportunity for choice and change in all we do. Third, fulfillment of the search for purpose is thwarted by a stunning fact: Out of more than a score of great civilizations in human history, modern Western civilization is the very first to have no agreed-upon answer to the question of the purpose of life. Thus ignorance, confusion—and longing—surround this topic more now than at almost any time in history. The trouble is that, as modern people, we have too much to live with and too little to live for. Some feel they have time but not enough money; others feel they have money but not enough time. But for most of us, in the midst of material and philosophical plenty, we have spiritual poverty. As a result, many people simply make do by constructing their own sense of purpose as best they can.

VISIONARIES WHO ADD VALUE

This book is for all who long to find and fulfill the purpose of their lives. It argues that this purpose can be found only when we discover the specific purpose for which we were created and to which we are called. The great Creator alone knows our reason for being and calls us into a life of purpose. As we human beings rise to the call of our Creator, we become sub-creators, entering into our own creativity, artistry, and entrepreneurship as made in his image—thus adding to the rich fruitfulness of the universe. Answering the call of our Creator is "the ultimate why" for living, the highest source of purpose in human existence, because it literally transforms us into "entrepreneurs of life." Apart from such a calling, all hope of discovering purpose (as in the current talk of shifting "from success to significance") will end in disappointment. To be sure, calling is not what it is commonly thought to be. It has to be dug out from under the rubble of ignorance and confusion. And, uncomfortably, it often flies directly in the face of our human inclinations. But nothing short of God's call can ground and fulfill the truest human desire for purpose.

One place where the confusion is lifting is the growing understanding that purpose cannot be found in means, only ends. Capitalism, for all its creativity and fruitfulness, falls short when challenged to answer the question "Why?" By itself it is literally meaningless, in that it is only a mechanism, not a source of meaning. So too are politics, science, psychology, management, self-help techniques, and a host of other modern theories. What Tolstoy wrote of science applies to all of them: "Science is meaningless because it gives no answer to our question, the only question important to us, 'what shall we do and how shall we live?'" There is no answer outside a quest for purpose and no answer to the quest is deeper and more satisfying than answering the call.

What is meant by "calling"? *Calling is the truth that God calls us to himself so decisively that everything we are, everything we do, and everything we have is invested with a special devotion and dynamism lived out as a response to his summons and service.*

And what is meant by "entrepreneur of life"? The entrepreneur is the person who assumes the responsibility for a creative task, not as an assigned role, a routine function, or an inherited duty, but as a venture of faith, including risk and danger, in order to bring into the world something new and profitable to humankind. Called in this sense, and answering such a call by rising to it in faith, entrepreneurs of life use their talents and resources to be fruitful and bring added value into the world—quite literally making the invisible visible, the future present, the ideal real, the impossible an achievement, the desired an experience, the status quo dynamic, and the dream a fulfillment.

To be sure, there is much in life we did not choose and cannot change. At the beginning of life none of us decided the date of our birth, the color of our eyes, or the pedigree of our ancestry. And at the end we do not decide the day of our death or the weight of our legacy. In between there are a million and one circumstances over which we have no control. But we are still, always, essentially people of significance—men and women whose entrepreneurial capacity to exercise dominion, to assert influence, and to multiply fruitfulness is at the heart of our humanness.

To stress the entrepreneurial must not be confused with the heartless heresy that an individual is valuable only in so far as he or she is profitable. But it is to see, as philosopher Dallas Willard states, that all of us have "a unique eternal calling to count for good in God's great universe."

The artist Vincent van Gogh captured this expansive view of artistry and entrepreneurship when he wrote to his closest friend, Emile Berhard, just two years before his death. Van Gogh noted that Jesus of Nazareth lived "as a greater artist than all other artists, despising marble and clay as well as color, working in living flesh. That is to say, this matchless artist . . . made neither statues nor pictures nor books; he loudly proclaimed that he made . . . living men, immortals."

This truth—calling—has been a driving force in many of the greatest "leaps forward" in world history—the constitution of the Jewish nation at Mount Sinai, the birth of the Christian movement in Galilee, and the sixteenth-century Reformation and its incalculable impetus to the rise of the modern world, to name a few. Little wonder that the rediscovery of calling should be critical today, not least in satisfying the passion for purpose of millions of questing modern people.

For whom is this book written? For all who seek such purpose. For all, whether believers or seekers, who are open to the call of the most influential person in history—Jesus of Nazareth. In particular, this book is written for those who know that their source of purpose must rise above the highest of self-help humanist hopes and who long for their faith to have integrity and effectiveness in the face of all the challenges of the modern world.

The truth of calling has been as important to me in my journey of faith as any truth of the gospel of Jesus. In my early days of following Jesus, I was nearly swayed by others to head toward spheres of work they believed were worthier for everyone and right for me. If I was truly dedicated, they said, I should train to be a minister or a missionary.

I did not know it then, but the start of my search (and the genesis of this book) lay in a chance conversation in the 1960s, in the days before self-service gas stations. I had just had my car filled up with gas and enjoyed a marvelously rich conversation with the pump attendant. As I turned the key and the engine of the forty-year-old Austin Seven roared to life, a thought suddenly hit me with the force of an avalanche: This man was the first person I had spoken to in a week who was not a church member. I was in danger of being drawn into a religious ghetto.

Urged on all sides to see that, because I had come

to faith, my future must lie in the ministry, I had volunteered to work in a well-known church for nine months—and was miserable. To be fair, I admired the pastor and the people and enjoyed much of the work. But it just wasn't me. My passion was to relate my faith to the exciting and exploding secular world of early 1960s Europe, but there was little or no scope for that in the ministry. Ten minutes of conversation with a friendly gas pump attendant on a beautiful spring evening in Southampton, England, and I knew once and for all that I was not cut out to be a minister.

Needless to say, recognizing who we aren't is only the first step toward knowing who we are. Escape from a false sense of life-purpose is only liberating if it leads to a true one. Journalist Ambrose Bierce reached only halfway. "When I was in my twenties," he wrote, "I concluded one day that I was not a poet. It was the bitterest moment of my life."

Looking back on the years since my conversation at the gas station, I can see that calling was positive for me, not negative. Released from what was "not me," my discovery of my calling enabled me to find what I was. Having wrestled with the stirring saga of calling in history and having taken up the challenge of God's individual call to me, I have been mastered by this truth. God's call has become a sure beacon ahead of me and a blazing fire within me as I have tried to figure out my way and negotiate the challenges of the extraordinary times in which we live. The chapters that follow are not academic or theoretical; they have been hammered out on the anvil of my own experience.

Do you long to discover your own sense of purpose and fulfillment? Let me be plain. You will not find here a "one-page executive summary," a "how-to manual," a "twelve-step program," or a ready-made "game plan" for figuring out the rest of your life. What you will find may point you toward one of the most powerful and truly awesome truths that has ever arrested the human heart.

"In Ages of Faith," Alexis de Tocqueville observed, "the final aim of life is placed beyond life." That is what calling does. "Follow me," Jesus said two thousand years ago, and he changed the course of history. That is why calling provides the Archimedean point by which faith moves the world. That is why calling is the most comprehensive reorientation and the most profound motivation in human experience—the ultimate Why for living in all history. Calling begins and ends such ages and lives of faith by placing the final aim of life beyond the world where it was meant to be. Answering the call is the way to find and fulfill the central purpose of your life.

Do you have a reason for being, a focused sense of purpose in your life? Or is your life the product of shifting resolutions and the myriad pulls of forces outside yourself? Do you want to go beyond success to significance? Have you come to realize that self-reliance always falls short and that world-denying solutions provide no answer in the end?

LISTEN TO JESUS OF NAZARETH;
ANSWER HIS CALL.

2

❦

EVERYONE, EVERYWHERE, EVERYTHING

One evening in 1787 a young English Member of Parliament pored over papers by candle-light in his home beside the Houses of Parliament. Wilberforce had been asked to propose the abolition of the slave trade although almost all Englishmen thought the trade necessary, if nasty, and that economic ruin would follow if it stopped. Only a very few thought the slave trade wrong, evil."

So opened a fascinating lecture on William Wilberforce given by his biographer John Pollock at the National Portrait Gallery in London in 1996.

Wilberforce's research pressed him to excruciatingly clear conclusions. "So enormous, so dreadful," he told the House of Commons later, "so irremediable did the trade's wickedness appear that my own mind was completely made up for abolition. Let the consequences be what they would, I from this time determined that I would never rest until I had effected its abolition."

Amazingly, no great reformer in Western history is so little known as William Wilberforce. His success in suppressing the slave trade was described by Pollock as "the greatest moral achievement of the British people" and by historian G. M. Trevelyan as "one of the turning events in the history of the world." His success was also credited by another historian with saving England from the French Revolution and demonstrating the character that was to be the foundation of the Victorian age. An Italian diplomat who saw Wilberforce in Parliament in his later years recorded that "everyone contemplates this little old man . . . as the Washington of humanity."

Equally amazingly, Wilberforce's momentous accomplishments were achieved in the face of immense odds. As regards the man himself, Wilberforce was by all accounts an ugly little man with too long a nose, a relatively weak constitution, and a despised faith—"evangelicalism" or "enthusiasm." As regards the task, the practice of slavery was almost universally accepted and the slave trade was as important to the economy of the British Empire as the defense industry is to the United States today. As regards his opposition, it included powerful mercantile and colonial vested interests, such national heroes as Admiral Lord Nelson, and most of the royal family. And as regards his perseverance, Wilberforce kept on tirelessly for nearly fifty years before he accomplished his goal.

Perhaps most amazingly, William Wilberforce came within a hair's breadth of missing his grand calling altogether. His faith in Jesus Christ animated his lifelong passion for reform. At one stage he led or actively participated in sixty-nine different initiatives, several of world-shaping significance. But when Wilberforce came to faith through the "Great Change" that was his experience of conversion in 1785 at the age of twenty-five, his first reaction was to throw over politics for the ministry. He thought, as millions have thought before and since, that "spiritual" affairs are far more important than "secular" affairs.

Fortunately, a minister—John Newton, the converted slave trader who wrote "Amazing Grace"—persuaded Wilberforce that God wanted him to stay in politics rather than enter the ministry. "It's hoped and believed," Newton wrote, "that the Lord has raised you up for the good of the nation." After much prayer and thought, Wilberforce concluded that Newton was right. God was calling him to champion the liberty of the oppressed—as a Parliamentarian. "My walk," he wrote in his journal in 1788, "is a public one. My business is in the world; and I must mix in the assemblies of men, or quit the post which Providence seems to have assigned me."

CALLING—THE CORE

Sadly, for every follower of Christ who, like William Wilberforce, chooses not to elevate the spiritual at the expense of the secular, countless others fall for the temptation. Wilberforce's celebrated "near miss" therefore leads us to the heart of understanding the character of calling and the first of two grand distortions that cripple it. Earlier, I defined the notion of calling this way: *Calling is the truth that God calls us to himself so decisively that everything we are, everything we do, and everything we have is invested with a special devotion, dynamism, and direction lived out as a response to his summons and service.*

Now it is time to unpack that truth further, beginning with four essential strands in the biblical notion of calling that we must always hold.

First, calling has a simple and straightforward meaning. In the Old Testament the Hebrew word that has been translated as "call" usually has the same everyday meaning as our English word. Human beings call to each other, to God, and to animals. Animals, too, can call. (The psalmist, for example, wrote that God "provides food for the cattle and for the young ravens when they call.") Under the pressure of theology and history, the term *call* has traveled a long way from this simple beginning, but this straightforward sense and its obvious relational setting should never be lost. When you "call" on the phone, for example, you catch someone's ear for a season.

Second, calling has another important meaning in the Old Testament. To call means to name, and to name means to call into being or to make. Thus in the first chapter of Genesis, "God called the light 'day' and the darkness he called 'night.'" This type of calling is far more than labeling, hanging a name-tag on something to identify it. Such decisive, creative naming is a form of making. Thus when God called Israel, he named and thereby constituted and created Israel his people. Thus "naming-calling," a very different thing from name-calling, is the fusion of being and becoming.

Third, calling gains a further characteristic meaning in the New Testament. It is almost a synonym for salvation. In this context, calling is overwhelmingly God's calling people to himself as followers of Christ. Just as God called Israel to him as his people, so Jesus called his disciples. The body of Jesus' followers as a whole is the community of the "called-out ones" (the origin of *ecclesia,* the Greek word for "church"). This decisive calling by God is salvation. Those who are called by God are first chosen and later justified and glorified. But calling is the most prominent and accessible of these four initiatives of God. Not surprisingly it often stands for salvation itself, and the common description of disciples of Jesus is not "Christian" but "followers of the Way."

Fourth, calling has a vital, extended meaning in the New Testament that flowers more fully in the later history of the church. God calls people to himself, but this call is no casual suggestion. He is so awe-inspiring and his summons so commanding that only one response is appropriate—a response as total and universal as the authority of the Caller.

Thus in the New Testament, as Jesus calls his followers to himself, he also calls them to other things and tasks: to peace, to fellowship, to eternal life, to suffering, and to service. But deeper even than these particular things, discipleship, which implies "everyone, everywhere, and in everything," is the natural and rightful response to the lordship of Christ. As Paul wrote the followers of Christ in the little town of Colosse, "Whatever you do, work at it with all your heart, as working for the Lord, not for men."

In short, calling in the Bible is a central and dynamic theme that becomes a metaphor for the life of faith itself. To limit the word, as some insist, to a few texts and to a particular stage in salvation is to miss the forest for the trees. To be a disciple of Jesus is to be a "called one" and so to become "a follower of the Way."

The third and fourth strands of the meaning of calling are the basis for the vital distinction elaborated later in history—between primary and secondary calling. *Our primary calling as followers of Christ is by him, to him, and for him.* First and foremost we are called to Someone (God), not to something (such as motherhood, politics, or teaching) or to somewhere (such as the inner city or Outer Mongolia).

Our secondary calling, considering who God is as sovereign, is that everyone, everywhere, and in everything should think, speak, live, and act entirely for him. We can therefore properly say as a matter of secondary calling that we are called to home-making or to the practice of law or to art history. But these and other things are always the secondary, never the primary calling. They are "callings" rather than the "calling." They are our personal answer to God's address, our response to God's summons. Secondary callings matter, but only because the primary calling matters most.

This vital distinction between primary and secondary calling carries with it two challenges—first, to hold the two together and, second, to ensure that they are kept in the right order. In other words, if we understand calling, we must make sure that first things remain first and the primary calling always comes before the secondary calling. But we

must also make sure that the primary calling leads
without fail to the secondary calling. The church's
failure to meet these challenges has led to the two
grand distortions that have crippled the truth of calling. We may call them the "Catholic distortion"
and the "Protestant distortion."

THE "CATHOLIC DISTORTION"

The truth of calling means that for followers of
Christ, "everyone, everywhere, and in everything" lives the whole of life as a response to
God's call. Yet this holistic character of calling
has often been distorted to become a form of
dualism that elevates the spiritual at the expense
of the secular. The first distortion may be called
the "Catholic distortion" because it rose in the
Catholic era and is the majority position in the
Catholic tradition.

The earliest clear example of the Catholic distortion is found in *Demonstration of the Gospel*
by Eusebius, bishop of Caesarea, written just before

the "conversion" of Constantine in A.D. 312 and the Roman Empire. Eusebius argues that Christ gave "two ways of life" to his church. One is the "perfect life"; the other is "permitted." The perfect life is spiritual, dedicated to contemplation and reserved for priests, monks, and nuns; the permitted life is secular, dedicated to action and open to such tasks as soldiering, governing, farming, trading, and raising families. Whereas those following the perfect life "appear to die to the life of mortals, to bear with them nothing earthly but their body, and in mind and spirit to have passed to heaven," those following the "more humble, more human" permitted life have "a kind of secondary grade of piety."

Higher vs. lower, sacred vs. secular, perfect vs. permitted, contemplation vs. action . . . the dualism and elitism in this view need no underscoring. Sadly this "two-tier" or "double-life" view of calling flagrantly perverted biblical teaching by narrowing the sphere of calling and excluding most Christians from its scope. It also dominated later Christian thinking. For example, both Augustine and Thomas Aquinas praised the work of farmers, craftsmen, and merchants but always elevated the contemplative life (*vita contemplativa*) over the active life (*vita activa*). The active life was depicted as second class, a matter of necessity; the contemplative life as first class, a matter of freedom. In short, Aquinas wrote, the life of contemplation was "simply better than the life of action." For most people in Christendom in medieval times, the term *calling* was reserved for priests, monks, and nuns. Everyone else just had "work." Even today, when one can find examples of Catholics recovering a more holistic view of calling, "answering the call" is commonly the jargon for becoming a priest or nun.

Into that long-established, rigidly hierarchical, and spiritually aristocratic world, Martin Luther's *The Babylonian Captivity of the Church* exploded like a thunderclap in 1520. Writing as an Augustinian monk himself, Luther recommended the abolition of all orders and abstention from all vows. Why? Because the contemplative life has no warrant in the Scriptures; it reinforces hypocrisy and arrogance; and it engenders "conceit and a contempt of the common Christian life."

But even these radical-sounding proposals pale beside the next paragraph Luther wrote: "The works of monks and priests, however holy and arduous they be, do not differ one whit in the sight of God from the works of the rustic laborer in the field or the woman going about her household tasks, but that all works are measured before God by faith alone. . . . Indeed, the menial housework of a manservant or maidservant is often more acceptable to God than all the fastings and other works of a monk or priest, because the monk or priest lacks faith."

If all that a believer does grows out of faith and is done for the glory of God, then all dualistic distinctions are demolished. There is no higher/ lower, sacred/secular, perfect/permitted, contemplative/ active, or first class/second class. Calling is the premise of Christian existence itself. Calling means that everyone, everywhere, and in everything fulfills his or her (secondary) callings in response to God's (primary) calling. For Luther, the peasant and the merchant—for us, the business person, the teacher, the factory worker, and the television anchor—can do God's work (or fail to do it) just as much as the minister and the missionary.

Little wonder that the cultural implications of recovering true calling were explosive. Calling gave to everyday work a dignity and spiritual significance under God that dethroned the primacy of leisure and contemplation. Calling gave to humble people and ordinary tasks an investment of equality that shattered hierarchies and was a vital impulse toward democracy. Calling gave to such practical things as work, thrift, and long-term planning a reinforcement that made them powerfully influential in the rise of modern capitalism. Calling gave to the endeavor to make Christ Lord of every part of life a fresh force that transformed not only the churches but also the worldviews and cultures of the Reformation countries. Calling gave to the idea of "talents" a new meaning, so that they were no longer seen purely as spiritual gifts and graces but as natural and a matter of giftedness in the modern sense of the term.

NO CALLING WITHOUT A CALLER

"Jobs are not big enough for people. It's not just the assembly line worker whose job is too small for his spirit, you know. A job like mine, if you really put your spirit into it, you would sabotage immediately. You don't dare. So you absent your spirit from it. My mind has been so divorced from my job, except as a source of income, it's really absurd."

The speaker, Norah Watson, was a twenty-eight-year-old Pennsylvania writer who worked for an institution that published health-care literature. She was being interviewed by Studs Terkel for his book *Working*, a series of interviews with ordinary people who "talk about what they do all day and how they feel about what they do."

Terkel realized, as he set out in his interviews, that working is about the search for daily meaning in the struggle for daily bread. Most people, he found, live somewhere between a grudging acceptance of their job and an active dislike of it. But a recurring theme in the interviews is a yearning for a sense of meaning that comes when calling precedes and overarches work and career.

Norah Watson's frustration was not fueled simply by her job. It came as much from the contrast between her experience and her father's, as a pastor in a small mountain town in western Pennsylvania. "My father was a preacher," she explained. "I didn't like what he was doing, but it was his vocation. That was the good part of it. It was not just go to work in the morning and punch a time clock. It was a profession of himself. I expected work to be like that. . . . For all that was bad about my father's vocation, he showed me it was possible to fuse your life to your work. . . . There's nothing I would enjoy more than a job that was so meaningful that I brought it home."

Norah Watson's pained candor about her work would not speak for those at the bottom of the totem pole or for those at the top. To the former such analysis would be an unaffordable luxury. They work to put bread on the table. To the latter it would be redundant; their work is often as satisfying and handsomely remunerated as work can get. But Norah Watson speaks for countless people in modern society who face the Catch-22 of modern work. Neither work nor career can be fully satisfying without a deeper sense of calling—but "calling" itself is empty and indistinguishable from work unless there is *someone* who calls.

The same dilemma is equally striking at the theoretical level. For example, one contemporary bestseller argues—admirably—that we need to "make a life, not just a living," and that to do this we need to inject "values and vocation" back into the world of work. With such a "new paradigm," the book claims, work can become "a vehicle for transformation," personally and socially.

On what basis? The author dusts off the word *calling* to give a sense of meaning and high purpose to work. But what is calling for those, like her, who believe that there is no personal God to call? Her answer is to redefine vocation as "the call, the summons of that which needs doing."

What sort of answer is this? Modern work lacks meaning. Meaning comes with a sense of calling. But calling is only the summons of what needs doing. So the answer to meaningless work is the requirement to do what needs doing—often more meaningless work. Tell that to the paper pusher in the government office or the widget maker on the factory assembly line. Work that feels meaningless is transformed, she says, by being made into work "which needs doing." Stripped of the semantic magic of the word *calling*, the solution is circular. It solves nothing and leaves us where we started.

The hollowness of the argument comes out most clearly in the author's laudable attempt to propose an answer to "workaholism." "The workaholic," she writes, "like an alcoholic, is indiscriminate in his compulsion. He attempts to find meaning by working. The individual with vocation, on the other hand, finds meaningful work."

But again notice the sleight of hand. True vocation, when there is a Caller to call, is truly different from workaholism. But the difference between the workaholic who wants to "find meaning by work" and the worker whose "vocation" is to do "that which needs doing" is too slight for comfort. A better and more honest solution is needed.

THE "PROTESTANT DISTORTION"

Such contortions in the modern effort to reinvest work with dignity pinpoint the second of the two grand distortions that cripple calling—the "Protestant distortion." Indeed, these contortions are a direct result of the Protestant distortion. Whereas the Catholic distortion is a spiritual form of dualism, elevating the spiritual at the expense of the secular, the Protestant distortion is a secular form of dualism, elevating the secular at the expense of the spiritual.

Under the pressure of the modern world, the Protestant distortion is more extreme. It severs the secular from the spiritual altogether and reduces vocation to an alternative word for work. In so doing, it completely betrays the purpose of calling and, ironically, activates a counter-reaction that swings back to the Catholic distortion again. Better, it would seem, the dualism of making calling purely spiritual than the dualism of making calling purely secular.

The seeds of the Protestant distortion can be traced right back to the Puritans themselves. Overall, the Puritans were magnificent champions of calling. Like the earlier reformers, the best and clearest thinking of them never split the primary call ("by God, to God, for God") from the secondary call ("everyone, everywhere, in everything").

John Calvin, it is true, does come close to speaking of a calling as equated with work. For Martin Luther, believers answer the call when through faith they serve God in their work, but Calvin sometimes speaks more boldly in equating calling and work. For both reformers, there were some occupations that could not be from God and, therefore, could never really be viewed as vocations. But Calvin in his tract "Against the Libertines" refers even to these illegitimate occupations as vocations—although sarcastically. "Let a brothel keeper . . . ply his trade . . . let a thief steal boldly, for each is pursuing his vocation."

But what may have been a latent imbalance earlier grows steadily in the Puritan era into a full-grown distortion. Slowly such words as *work, trade, employment,* and *occupation* came to be used interchangeably with calling and vocation. As this happened, the guidelines for callings shifted; instead of being directed by the commands of God, they were seen as directed by duties and roles in society. Eventually the day came when faith and calling were separated completely. The original demand that each Christian should have a calling was boiled down to the demand that each citizen should have a job.

Finally, the wheel came full circle. Callings had become jobs and jobs had become corrupt, so the radical seventeenth-century Protestant group, the Diggers, called for the abolition of callings altogether. Gerrard Winstanley, in a 1650 tract in England, wrote: "The judges and law officers buy and sell justice for money, and wipe their mouth like Solomon's whore and say 'It is my calling,' and are never troubled at it." Thus, ironically, whereas the reformers had set out the rediscovery of "calling" as a consequence of true faith, some of their spiritual descendants called for the "abolition of call-ings"—also as a consequence of true faith.

To be sure, the tight logic of the Diggers was too radical for most people. In the broad mainstream of European and American life, the steady seculariz-ation of calling continued apace. Slowly but surely secondary callings swallowed up the primary calling.

Is there a way back from the disaster of the Protestant distortion? At least two things are re-quired: the debunking of the notion of calling with-out a Caller and the restoring of the primacy of the primary calling.

First, we must resolutely refuse to play the word games that pretend calling means anything with-out a Caller—and we must not allow people to play such games on us. A hundred years ago Friedrich Nietzsche rightly scorned those who said, "God is dead" and went on living exactly the same as before. One of those in his sights was nov-elist George Eliot, who wrote, "God is 'inconceiv-able' and immortality 'unbelievable,' but duty is nonetheless 'peremptory and absolute.'"

Nietzsche derided such people as "odious windbags of progressive optimism" who think it possible to have Christian morality without Christian faith. "They are rid of the Christian God," he wrote in *Twilight of the Idols,* "and now believe all the more firmly that they must cling to the Christian morality. . . . When one gives up the Christian faith, one pulls the right to Christian morality out from under one's feet."

What is true of morality is true of calling too. In C. S. Lewis's homespun picture, those who still conjure meaning out of calling when they do not believe there is a Caller are as silly as "the woman in the first war who said that if there were a bread shortage it would not bother her house because they always ate toast." If there is no Caller, there are no callings—only work.

Second, and more positively, we must restore the primary calling to its primary place by restoring the worship that is its setting and the dedication to Jesus that is its heart. There is no surer guide here than the devotional writer Oswald Chambers. "Beware of anything that competes with loyalty to Jesus Christ," he wrote. "The greatest competitor of devotion to Jesus is service for Him. . . . The one aim of the call of God is the satisfaction of God, not a call to do something for Him."

Do we enjoy our work, love our work, virtually worship our work so that our devotion to Jesus is off-center? Do we put our emphasis on service, or usefulness, or being productive in working for God—at his expense? Do we strive to prove our own significance? To make a difference in the world? To carve our names in marble on the monuments of time?

The call of God blocks the path of all such deeply human tendencies. We are not primarily called to do something or go somewhere; we are called to Someone. We are not called first to special work but to God. The key to answering the call is to be devoted to no one and to nothing above God himself. As Chambers said, "The men and women Our Lord sends out on His enterprises are the ordinary human stuff, plus dominating devotion to Himself wrought by the Holy Spirit." The most frequent phrase in his writings: "Be absolutely His."

In sum, we must avoid the two distortions by keeping the two callings together, stressing the primary calling to counter the Protestant distortion and secondary callings to counter the Catholic distortion. Whereas dualism cripples calling, a holistic understanding releases its power—the passion to be God's concentrates the energy of all who answer the call.

Do you want to accept a challenge that will be the integrating dynamic of your whole life? One that will engage your loftiest thoughts, your most dedicated exertions, your deepest emotions, all your abilities and resources, to the last step you take and the last breath you breathe? Do you want to be his, entirely his, at all costs his, and forever his so that secondary things remain so and first things are always first?

LISTEN TO JESUS OF NAZARETH;
ANSWER HIS CALL.

3

DO WHAT YOU ARE

Yehudi Menuhin, the renowned maestro and violinist, has held audiences all over the world spellbound with his conducting and virtuoso playing. Like many great musicians, his gifts were precocious. He made his violin debut in San Francisco at the age of seven and launched his worldwide career at the age of twelve with a historic concert at Carnegie Hall. In his memoirs, *Unfinished Journey,* Menuhin tells the story of how he began his long love affair with the violin.

From the time he was three years old, Menuhin's parents frequently took him to concerts in New York, where he heard the concertmaster and first violinist Louis Persinger. When Persinger broke into solo passages, little Yehudi, sitting with his parents up in the gallery, was enchanted.

"During one such performance," Menuhin wrote, "I asked my parents if I might have a violin for my fourth birthday and Louis Persinger to teach me to play it."

Apparently his wish was granted. A family friend gave the little boy a violin, but it was a toy one, made of metal with metal strings. Yehudi Menuhin was only four. He could hardly have had the arms and fingers to do justice to a full-sized violin, but he was furious.

"I burst into sobs, threw it on the ground and would have nothing to do with it." Reflecting years later, Menuhin said he realized he wanted nothing less than the real thing because, "I did know instinctively that to play was to be."

Stories like that are common in the lives of creative artists. Artie Shaw, a famous clarinetist in the old Big Band days, shared his heart with an interviewer. "Maybe twice in my life I reached what I wanted to. Once we were playing 'These Foolish

Things' and at the end the band stops and I play a little cadenza. That cadenza—no one can do it better. Let's say it's five bars. That's a very good thing to have done in a lifetime. An artist should be judged by his best, just as an athlete. Pick out my one or two best things and say, 'That's what we did: all the rest was rehearsal.'"

John Coltrane, the saxophonist who played for Dizzie Gillespie and Miles Davis, said something very similar. In the early 1950s "Trane" nearly died of a drug overdose in San Francisco, and when he recovered he quit drugs and drinking and came to put his faith in God. Some of his best jazz came after that, including "A Love Supreme," an ardent thirty-two minute outpouring to thank God for his blessing and offer him Coltrane's very soul.

After one utterly extraordinary rendition of "A Love Supreme," Coltrane stepped off the stage, put down his saxophone, and said simply, *"Nunc dimittis."* (These are the opening Latin words for the ancient prayer of Simeon, sung traditionally at evening prayers: "Lord, now lettest thou thy servant depart in peace, for mine eyes have seen thy salvation.") Coltrane felt he could never play the piece more perfectly. If his whole life had been lived for that passionate thirty-two-minute jazz prayer, it would have been worth it. He was ready to go.

WHAT DO YOU HAVE THAT WAS NOT GIVEN YOU?

"To play was to be," said Yehudi Menuhin. "All the rest was rehearsal," said Artie Shaw. *"Nunc dimittis,"* said John Coltrane. Somehow we human beings are never happier than when we are expressing the deepest gifts that are truly us. And often we get a revealing glimpse of these gifts early in life. Graham Greene wrote in *The Power and the Glory,* "There is always one moment in childhood when the door opens and lets the future in." Countless examples could be added to these stories, but they all point to another crucial aspect of calling—*God normally calls us along the line of our giftedness, but the purpose of giftedness is stewardship and service, not selfishness.*

Giftedness does not stand alone in helping us discern our callings. It lines up in response to God's call alongside other factors, such as family heritage, our own life opportunities, God's guidance, and our unquestioning readiness to do what he shows. But to focus on giftedness as a central way to discern calling reverses the way most people think. Usually when we meet someone for the first time, it isn't long before we ask, "What do you do?" And the answer comes, "I'm a lawyer," "I'm a truck driver," "I'm a teacher," or whatever.

Far more than a name or a place of birth, a job helps us place a person on the map in our minds. After all, work, for most of us, determines a great part of our opportunity for significance and the amount of good we are able to produce in a lifetime. Besides, work takes up so many of our waking hours that our jobs come to define us and give us our identities. We become what we do.

Calling reverses such thinking. A sense of calling should precede a choice of job and career, and the main way to discover calling is along the line of what we are each created and gifted to be.

Instead of, "You are what you do," calling says: "Do what you are." As the great Christian poet Gerard Manley Hopkins wrote in his poem about kingfishers and dragonflies, "What I do is me: for that I came." Albert Einstein, even as a teenager, had theoretical physics and mathematics in his sights. He wrote in a homework essay in Aarau, Switzerland, "That is quite natural; one always likes to do the things for which one has ability."

There is, to be fair, a growing trend toward fitting jobs to people. "Suit yourself—the secret of career satisfaction" one book promises. But many of these approaches are inadequate compared to calling. First, the more secular approaches tend to use very general "personality types" in their testing. So the results are too broad to be specific for individuals, and they are more about general personality traits than about the specific gifts of individuals.

Second, even the more clearly Christian approaches often suffer from weaknesses. Some use testing that concentrates on spiritual gifts and ignores natural gifts. This allows the testers, usually large churches, to use the results to direct people to employ their discovered gifts in their churches—thus diverting them from their callings in secular life and deepening the Catholic distortion further.

Others broaden the testing to discover both spiritual and natural gifts, but they divorce the discovery of giftedness from the worship and listening that is essential to calling—thus deepening the Protestant distortion further. The result is a heightened awareness of giftedness, but the emphasis on giftedness leads toward selfishness rather than stewardship. Archbishop William Temple underscored this danger sternly. To make the choice of career or profession on selfish grounds, without a true sense of calling, is "probably the greatest single sin any young person can commit, for it is the deliberate withdrawal from allegiance to God of the greatest part of time and strength."

In the biblical understanding of giftedness, gifts are never really ours or for ourselves. We have nothing that was not given us. Our gifts are ultimately God's, and we are only "stewards"—

responsible for the prudent management of property that is not our own. This is why our gifts are always "ours for others," whether in the community of Christ or the broader society outside, especially the neighbor in need.

This is also why it is wrong to treat God as a grand employment agency, a celestial executive searcher to find perfect fits for our perfect gifts. The truth is not that God is finding us a place for our gifts but that God has created us and our gifts for a place of his choosing—and we will only be ourselves when we are finally there.

This theme of the wider purpose of gifts was unambiguous to the Puritans. John Cotton, for example, was an eminent seventeenth-century minister and the architect of New England congregationalism. Educated at Trinity and Emmanuel Colleges, Cambridge, he preached the famous farewell sermon "God's Promise to His Plantation" at the sailing of the *Arbella* in 1630. Three years later, he came to the New World himself. His sermon "Christian Calling" is a stirring seven-point exposition on the subject.

Cotton gives three criteria for choosing a job. The top criterion is that "it be a warrantable calling, wherein we may not only aim at our own, but at the public good." The other criteria are that we are gifted for the job and guided toward it by God—criteria that would surely supersede Cotton's first one on most people's list today. All who seek to follow Christ and to answer his call should pursue the key link between their giftedness and their calling, and use the best Christian books and tests on the subject. There is joy in fulfilling a calling that fits who we are and, like the pillar of cloud and fire, goes ahead of our lives to lead us.

But who are we? And what is our destiny? Calling insists that the answer lies in God's knowledge of what he has created us to be and where he is calling us to go. Our gifts and destiny do not lie expressly in our parents' wishes, our boss's plans, our peer group's pressures, our generation's prospects, or our society's demands. Rather, we each need to know our own unique design, which is God's design for us.

OURS FOR OTHERS

Not surprisingly, the focus on giftedness can be dangerous as well as wonderful. The encouragement to "do what we are" can be taken as a blank check for self-indulgence. But the strongest temptations always come along the line of the noblest truths, and that is the case here: The principle is tempting because it is true.

God does call us to "be ourselves" and "do what we are." But we are only truly "ourselves" and can only truly "do what we are" when we follow God's call. Giftedness that is "ours for others" is therefore not selfishness but service that is perfect freedom.

The danger, however, remains. So it is worth noting some distinctions made throughout history regarding calling, which help us balance giftedness and stewardship. In each case the temptation is to remember only the giftedness and forget the stewardship. But by keeping both in mind, we can steer surely by the principles of calling and avoid the pitfalls.

In all the discussion, the terms *calling* and *vocation* should be synonymous. One word simply comes from an Anglo-Saxon root and the other from a Latin root. Beware of those who make "vocation" different from "calling." If "vocation" is ever distinguished from "calling" and used to refer to the clergy, it is a sure sign of the Catholic distortion; if "vocation" is distinguished from "calling" and used to refer to employment and occupation, it betrays the presence of the Protestant distortion.

First, we must remember the distinction between *the individual* (or *particular*) *calling* and *the corporate* (or *general*) *calling*. Selfishness prefers the first, but stewardship respects both. The individual calling is that part of our life-response to God that we make as unique individuals. As we have seen, our individual callings are unique simply because each of us is unique. The corporate calling, on the other hand, is that part of our life-response to God that we undertake in common with all other followers of Christ. For example, all followers of Christ are called to be holy and to be peacemakers—simply by virtue of being followers of Christ.

Our corporate calling is vital because it prevents calling from developing into an excessive individualism. Individual callings should complement, not contradict, the corporate calling. If there is any disagreement, the corporate calling as set out in Scripture should take precedence. Anyone citing his or her individual calling as grounds for rejecting the church's corporate calling is self-deluded. Characteristically, the Puritans thought about corporate calling as much as individual calling. William Perkins, the dean of Puritan writers on vocation, counseled that "every calling must be fitted to the man and every man fitted to his calling." Both halves of the rule are necessary, he said, "for when men are out of their proper callings in any society it is as much as if a joint were out of place in the body."

Second, we must remember the distinction between *a later, special calling* and *our original, ordinary calling*. Again, selfishness prefers the first, but stewardship respects both. A special calling refers to those tasks and missions laid on individuals through a direct, specific, supernatural communication from God. Ordinary calling, on the

other hand, is the believer's sense of life-purpose
and life-task in response to God's primary call,
"follow me," even when there is no direct, specific,
supernatural communication from God about a
secondary calling. In other words, ordinary calling can be seen in our responsibility to exercise a
high degree of "capitalist-style" enterprise about
how we live our lives. For example, the servants
in Jesus' parable of the talents and pounds were
assessed according to how they "got on with it"
when the master was away. In this sense no follower of Christ is without a calling, for we all have
an original calling even if we do not all have a
later, special calling. And, of course, some people
have both.

This distinction has practical consequences.
Many Christians make the mistake of elevating a
special calling or of talking as if everyone needed
a special call for every task. ("Were you called to
this job?") Some use the word *calling* piously
regarding all their decisions, thinking it is the
word to use, when in fact they have not had any
special call. To the surprise of both groups, there

is not a single instance in the New Testament of God's special call to anyone into a paid occupation or into the role of a religious professional. Others feel that, without a special call, they have had no call at all. So they wait around for guidance and become passive, excusing themselves by saying they have had "no call." But all they are doing is confusing the two types of call and burying their real talent in the napkin in the ground.

Needless to say, the very notion of a special call by God often betrays the fact that something is awry in understanding the original call. This tension is sharpest in the prophet—the prophet is specially called to critique and challenge the people of God when they have forgotten or betrayed their original calling.

Thus Moses confronted the people of God over the golden calf, Elijah over the prophets of Baal, Jesus over legalism and hypocrisy, Martin Luther over the distortion of faith, and Karl Barth and Dietrich Bonhoeffer over the idolatry of nationalism. Such prophetic critiques were often delivered with outrage, but they were not denials of the chosenness of those attacked. On the contrary, the purpose of prophetic critique is restoration, not dismissal. The prophets were specially called and their prophetic messages were special calls to bring God's people back to the original calling from which they had fallen away.

Third, we must remember the distinction between something being *central* to our calling and something being *peripheral*. Again, selfishness prefers the first, but stewardship regards both. Many people use the word *calling* only for the core of our giftedness. They speak as if we should all be able to specify our callings as a single task expressed in a single sentence. But both people and life are richer than that, and calling is comprehensive, not partial. We need to remember that calling has multiple dimensions and includes our relationships. Martin Luther, for example, was among other things husband to his wife, father to his daughter, pastor to his congregation, professor to his students, and subject to his prince.

This distinction is important because it is easy to become spoiled if we concentrate on the core of our giftedness—as if the universe existed only to fulfill our gifts. But it is also easy to become discouraged by making the same mistake. We live in a fallen world, and the core of our gifts may not be fulfilled in our lives on earth. If there had been no Fall, all our work would have naturally and fully expressed who we are and exercised the gifts we have been given. But after the Fall this is not so. Work is now partly creative and partly cursed. Thus to find work now that perfectly fits our callings is not a right, but a blessing. Those in modern societies who are middle class or higher can probably find such a fulfilling match between calling and work. But for many others today, and probably for most people in most societies, there is no happy match between work and calling. Work is a necessity for survival. Even the almost universally recognized artistic genius like Michelangelo once complained: "having seen, as I said, that the times are contrary to my art, I do not know if I have any hope of further salary."

This tension created by the Fall lies behind the

notion of "tentmaking." Needless to say, there was
no advertised job that was perfect for Paul's calling:
"Apostle to the Gentiles: $50,000 per annum." So
Paul, not wishing to depend on wealthy Corinthian
patrons, earned money by making tents. Doubtless
he made his tents well because they too were made
to the glory of God. But tentmaking was never the
heart of Paul's calling, it was only a *part,* as all of
life is. As a part of our calling such "tentmaking"
at worst is work that *frustrates* us because it takes
time we wish to spend on things more central. But
at best it is work that frees us to get to that which
is central. By contrast, whatever is the heart of our
calling is work that *fulfills* us because it employs
our deepest gifts.

The difference is impossible to mistake. George
Foreman, flamboyant heavyweight champion of
the world and a Baptist preacher says, "Preaching
is my calling. Boxing for me is only moonlighting
in the same way Paul made tents."

Fourth, we must remember the distinction between the *clarity* of calling and the *mystery* of
calling. Again selfishness prefers the first, but

stewardship regards both. To the extent that through worship, listening to God, and discovering our giftedness we grasp what God is calling us to be and do, there will be a proper clarity in our sense of calling. But to the extent that we blithely rush to be explicit, we betray our modern arrogance and forget the place of mystery in God's dealing with us. Oswald Chambers even said, writing of a special call:

> If you can tell where you got the call of God and all about it, I question whether you have ever had a call. The call of God does not come like that, it is much more supernatural. The realization of it in a man's life may come with a sudden thunderclap or with a gradual dawning, but in whatever way it comes it comes with the undercurrent of the supernatural, something that cannot be put into words.

Can you state your identity in a single sentence? No more should you necessarily be able to state your calling in a single sentence. At best you can specify only a part of it. And even that clarity may have to be qualified. In many cases a clear sense of calling comes only through a time of searching, including trial and error. And what may be clear to us in our twenties may be far more mysterious in our fifties because God's complete designs for us are never fully understood, let alone fulfilled, in this life.

William Wilberforce's 1787 journal entry, setting down his "two great objects," is perhaps the simplest and most stunning personal mission statement in history. But it would be wrong to hold it up as a model for all. Wilberforce was young, his sense of calling was clear, and he pursued that calling for the rest of his life almost as if he were running in a straight line.

Aleksandr Solzhenitsyn, a living legend in the twentieth century as a one-man resistance movement to totalitarianism, represents a very different way. When he was fifty-five and near the climax of his titanic struggle with the Soviets, with twenty more years of his writing projects still to be achieved, his sense of calling was passionate:

The one worrying thing was that I might not be given time to carry out the whole scheme. I felt as though I was about to fill a space in the world that was meant for me and had long awaited me, a mold, as it were, made for me alone, but discerned by me only this very moment. I was a molten substance, impatient, unendurably impatient, to pour into my mold, to fill it full, without air bubbles or cracks, before I cooled and stiffened.

But Solzhenitsyn's sense of calling had not always been so clear and passionate. Originally it had not been there at all because he did not know his Caller and barely knew his gift. "I drifted into literature unthinkingly," he said, ". . . and hate to think what sort of writer I would have become." But his sense of calling grew in his experiences of the Gulag, his deadly struggle to write, the miracle of his cure from cancer, his conversion through a Jewish follower of Jesus, and his deepening burden to put "the dying wish of the millions" on record.

Solzhenitsyn therefore exemplifies Sören Kierkegaard's observation that life is lived forward but understood backward. "Later," he wrote in *The Oak and the Calf,* "the true significance of what happened would inevitably become clear to me, and I would be numb with surprise. I have done many things in my life that conflicted with the great aims I had set myself—and something has always set me on the true path again."

Solzhenitsyn's conclusion, quoting another Russian writer, is a bracing reminder to all who yearn for calling to be always simple and clear. "Many lives have a mystical sense, but not everyone reads it aright. More often than not it is given to us in cryptic form, and when we fail to decipher it, we despair because our lives seem meaningless. The secret of a great life is often a man's success in deciphering the mysterious symbols vouchsafed to him, understanding them and so learning to walk in the true path."

Do you want the best and most wonderful gifts God has given you to decay, spent on your own self? Or do you want them to be set free to come into their own as you link your profoundest abilities with your neighbor's need and the glory of God?

LISTEN TO JESUS OF NAZARETH;
ANSWER HIS CALL.

CHAPTER

4

❦

THE AUDIENCE OF ONE

July 27, 1881, was the happiest day in the life of Andrew Carnegie. A Scottish weaver's son, he had risen from a Pittsburgh "bobbin boy" at $1.20 a week to America's "King of Steel," "the Industrial Napoleon," "the *Homo Croesus Americanus,*" "St. Andrew" (Mark Twain's nickname)— and one of the world's most fabled rich men. He was always proud to be called "the star-spangled Scotchman," and he had set his heart on a triumphal return to Dunfermline, the city of his birth in the east of Scotland. "What Benares is to the Hindu, Mecca to the Mohammedan, Jerusalem to the Christians, all that Dunfermline is to me," he purred as he saw the city from the Ferry Hills above it.

Carnegie's trip had been long planned. With his mother and a select group of friends, he crossed the Atlantic from New York, set out from Brighton on the south coast of England, and slowly traveled north to Scotland and Dunfermline in a carriage that was royally built and furnished. At four o'clock in the afternoon, the coach and four rolled up St. Leonard's Street, greeted by banners reading "Welcome Carnegie, generous son" and passing the flags of Scotland, England, and the United States.

Then the official parade began, led by the Lord Provost, the guilds, and town councilors in their carriages. The procession passed the little stone cottage where Carnegie had been born and a similar cottage nearby from which his poverty-stricken family had fled to Pittsburgh thirty-three years earlier.

The climax of the day was Carnegie's bestowal of a new, handsome public library on the city of his birth, the first such bequest outside the United States. But long before then, his mother Margaret, who throughout the entire trip had ridden on top of the coach, had asked to sit inside so that she could weep freely but unseen on her day of triumph.

Homecomings, alumni reunions, visits to ancestral countries . . . most people can identify with the feelings of a native son returning home. But Andrew Carnegie's pride that day had another source too. Years earlier, when he was a young boy and he and his family lived in penury in Pittsburgh, he found his mother weeping in a moment of despair. Cradling her hands in his, he urged her not to cry and tried to console her.

"Some day I'll be rich," he assured her, "and we'll ride in a fine coach driven by four horses."

"That will do no good over here," his mother snorted, "if no one in Dunfermline can see us."

That was the moment when young Andrew solemnly resolved that someday he and his mother would make a grand entry into Dunfermline in a coach and four, and the whole town would witness it. For his mother's sake, he would "show them." A Pittsburgh audience would not be enough for that. He had to prove the Carnegie family's success before his hometown audience.

Needless to say, Andrew Carnegie was no poll-taking, crowd-pleasing politician. Early on he spoke of business as a game of "solitaire"; his favorite line was Robert Burns's "Thine own reproach alone do fear"; and his personal creed—Social Darwinism—gave him a ruthless streak never wholly offset by the legendary generosity of his philanthropy. But Carnegie was not simply the "robber baron," the entrepreneurial capitalist egotist of his enemy's attacks.

Among the softening factors was his evident desire to please. A special drawer in his desk was labeled "gratitude and sweet words," and one of his secretary's daily tasks was to cut out favorable comments from the press and file them for Carnegie's enjoyment. Above all, he longed to win the approval of the few audiences he valued—especially the city of his birth. "It's God's mercy I was born a Scotchman," Carnegie the atheist avowed with no sense of contradiction when he crossed the Scottish border on July 16. And then more straightforwardly: "Ah, you suit me, Scotia, and proud I am that I am your son." Unquestionably, Andrew Carnegie and his mother Margaret had "shown them."

A GYROSCOPE OR A GALLUP POLL?

The preceding story, which is told so well in Joseph Frazier Wall's biography *Andrew Carnegie,* highlights a vital point for understanding calling. When we discuss our plans and endeavors, we automatically think of notions like "aims," "ambition," "achievements," "assessment," and so on. But we often overlook the vital part of "audience."

Only madmen, geniuses, and supreme egotists do things purely for themselves. It is easy to buck a crowd, not too hard to march to a different drummer. But it is truly difficult—perhaps impossible—to march only to your own drumbeat. Most of us, whether we are aware of it or not, do things with an eye to the approval of some audience or other. The question is not whether we have an audience but which audience we have.

This observation underscores another vital feature of the truth of calling: *A life lived listening to the decisive call of God is a life lived before one audience that trumps all others—the Audience of One.*

In Genesis Abraham's call is to live a life of trust in God as he journeys before God. Usually God calls Abraham, but at one point he appears and says, "I am God Almighty; walk before me and be blameless." Behind the voice of God is the eye of God and behind the eye the face and behind the face the heart. To follow the call of God is therefore to live before the heart of God. It is to live life *coram deo* (before the heart of God) and thus to shift our awareness of audiences to the point where only the last and highest—God—counts.

Jesus intensifies this same emphasis. He reminds those he calls that their Father "knows" and "sees." God notes the sparrow hopping on the ground, and he numbers the very hairs of his followers' heads. Contrary to the universal human desire to parade virtue and to give in order to be recognized and honored, Jesus required that our good deeds be secret. "Then your Father, who sees what is done in secret, will reward you."

This stress on living before the Audience of One was prominent among the Puritans. John Cotton expands on the theme of audience. Quoting St. Paul's letter to the Ephesians, he describes the calling of servants as "not with eye-service as man-pleasers." Rather, he says, "we live by faith in our vocations, in that faith, in serving God, serves men, and in serving men, serves God." But is this language simply Puritan word play? Far from it. Living before the Audience of One transforms all our endeavors—"he doth it all comfortably though he meet with little encouragement from man, whereas an unbelieving heart would be discontented that he can find no acceptance, but all he doth is taken in the worst part."

That is why Christ-centered heroism does not need to be noticed or publicized. The greatest deeds are done before the Audience of One, and that is enough. Those who are seen and sung by the Audience of One can afford to be careless about lesser audiences.

When asked why he was not stung by a vicious attack from a fellow Member of Parliament, Winston Churchill replied, "If I respected him, I would care about his opinion. But I don't, so I don't." Similarly we who live before the Audience of One can say to the world: "I have only one audience. Before you I have nothing to prove, nothing to gain, nothing to lose."

Needless to say, the modern world is light-years from the Puritan world. We have moved from the "inner directed" world of the Puritans, in which calling acted as an inner compass, to the "other directed" world of modern society, in which our contemporaries are our real guides—and a roving radar ranges to pick up their cues. We see this in teenagers listening to their peers, women following the beguiling images of womanhood in magazines and designer fashions, politicians aping polls and slavishly following focus group findings, and pastors anxiously following the latest profiles of "seekers" and "generations." One large church pastor told me, "I'm haunted when I look into the eyes of my congregation and realize they are always only two weeks away from leaving for another church."

Curiously, the twentieth century, which began

with some of the strongest leaders in all history—some good like Winston Churchill and Franklin Roosevelt, many bad like Lenin and Stalin—ended with a weak style of leadership codependent on followership: the leader as panderer.

"I hear it said," Churchill remarked in a speech in the House of Commons on September 30, 1941, that "leaders should keep their ears to the ground. All I can say is that the British nation will find it very hard to look up to the leaders who are detected in that somewhat ungainly posture." "Nothing is more dangerous," he said another time, "than to live in the temperamental atmosphere of a Gallup Poll—always feeling one's pulse and taking one's temperature."

Though almost always impressive before audiences and sometimes dazzling, Churchill himself was described by his friend Violet Bonham Carter as being "as impervious to atmosphere as a diver in his bell." Similarly Harry Truman, whose presidency included such momentous decisions as the Marshall Plan and the first use of the atomic bomb, once said: "I wonder how far Moses would have gone if he had taken a poll in Egypt."

By contrast, as great a genius as Wolfgang Amadeus Mozart could write (in a letter to his father in 1778), "I am never in a good humor when I am in a town where I am quite unknown." Extreme examples of "other-direction" or "outside-in" thinking are easy to find and poke fun at. For instance, an old French story tells of a revolutionary sitting in a Paris cafe, who suddenly hears a disturbance outside. He jumps to his feet and cries, "There goes the mob. I am their leader. I must follow them." Churchill's friend and colleague (and later prime minister) David Lloyd George was famed for his acute sensitivity to public opinion. Lord Keynes was once asked what happened to Lloyd George when he was alone in the room. Keynes replied, "When Lloyd George is alone in the room there is nobody there."

Screen goddess Marlene Dietrich even issued recordings of her cabaret ovations—two sides of nothing but applause. Her biographer tells us that she frequently gathered friends to listen and insisted on playing both sides to Judy Garland and Noel Coward. "That was Rio," she told them solemnly, "That was Cologne. That was Chicago."

Such narcissism may be fatuous, but we are all affected by the overall shift. The Puritans lived as if they had swallowed gyroscopes; we modern Christians live as if we have swallowed Gallup polls. Or as Martin Luther King wrote in his *Letter from Birmingham Jail,* "in those days the church was not merely a thermometer that recorded the ideas and principles of popular opinion; it was a thermostat that transformed the mores of society." Leaders or panderers? Gyroscope or Gallup poll? Thermostat or thermometer? Only those who practice the presence of the Audience of One can hope to attain the former and escape the latter.

Growing awareness of the Audience of One has greatly helped me in the vicissitudes of my own calling. Part of my calling, as I have discovered it and tried to fulfill it, has been to make sense of the gospel to the world (as an apologist) and to make sense of the world to the church (as an analyst). I have sought to do both in a way that stands between high, specialized, academic knowledge and ordinary, popular thinking.

This attempt to bridge means that no single

human audience is my sole, natural audience. In fact, each audience sometimes scorns the effort to reach the other. No sooner does one side dismiss the effort as hopelessly "intellectual" than the other disdains it as "mere popularizing." So I find it a tremendous comfort as well as a continual challenge to remember that above and beyond the impossible-to-satisfy constituencies is the one audience that matters—the Audience of One.

To live before the Audience of One truly makes a demonstrable difference. The character and life of the great nineteenth-century Christian soldier General Charles Gordon, sometimes known as "Chinese Gordon" or "Gordon of Khartoum," is a striking example. In his book on the recapture of Sudan, Winston Churchill described General Gordon as "a man careless alike of the frowns of men or the smiles of women, of life or comfort, wealth or fame." But these words came almost directly from Gordon himself. "The more one sees of life," Gordon wrote, "the more one feels, in order to keep from shipwreck, the necessity of steering by the Polar Star, i.e. in a word leave to God alone, and never pay attention to the favors or smiles of man; if He smiles on you, neither the smile or frown of men can affect you."

General Gordon was eventually abandoned and left to die in the siege of Khartoum because of the moral cowardice of Prime Minister William Gladstone and his cabinet in London. His end at the hand of the Mahdi and his fanatical followers is legendary. But his calling-inspired strength was equally legendary throughout his entire life.

"Do you know, Gordon Pasha," snarled the cruel King John of Abyssinia in an earlier incident, "that I could kill you on the spot if I liked?"

"I am perfectly well aware of it, Your Majesty," Gordon replied. "Do so at once if it is your royal pleasure. I am ready."

"What, ready to be killed?"

"Certainly. I am always ready to die. . . ."

"Then my power has no terrors for you?" the king gasped.

"None whatever!" Gordon answered, and the king left him, amazed.

After Gordon's death John Bonar, a Scottish

friend, wrote to Gordon's brother. "What at once and always struck me was the way in which his oneness with God ruled all his actions and his mode of seeing things. I never knew one who seemed so much to 'endure as seeing Him who is invisible.'" Gordon, he concluded, seemed "to live with God, and for God."

General Charles Gordon, peerless military strategist, legendary commander, and mostly all-conquering victor, lived so closely before the Audience of One that when his time came, he had only a short step home. Like all for whom God's call is decisive, it could be said of him, "I live before the Audience of One. Before others I have nothing to prove, nothing to gain, nothing to lose."

Do you wish to be inner-directed rather than other-directed and truly make one audience decisive, the Audience of One?

LISTEN TO JESUS OF NAZARETH;
ANSWER HIS CALL.

CHAPTER

5

❦

DREAMERS OF THE DAY

So long as the exploits of his life are still told and retold, people will always be torn in response to the enigma of T. E. Lawrence, or "Lawrence of Arabia." For some, no amount of Lawrence's brilliance and bravery will ever divert their eyes from his darker side. Novelist Lawrence Durrell called him "a disgusting little thing." For others, all the innuendo in the world will never dim the qualities that made Lawrence such a hero. Winston Churchill described Lawrence as "one of the greatest beings alive in our time." John Buchan, author, statesman, and governor general of Canada, was no fool as a judge of men and women. His estimate was typical:

"I would have followed Lawrence to the end of the world."

Even the spin-offs from T. E. Lawrence have been inspiring. Arguably, the Oscar-winning epic *Lawrence of Arabia* is one of the two greatest films of all time—along with Orson Welles's *Citizen Kane*. Certainly, it is the best film of director David Lean, who himself has been described as "the poet of the far horizon." Steven Spielberg is only the best known of those who credit their entry into filmmaking to this film. "I was inspired the first time I saw *Lawrence*. It made me feel puny. It still makes me feel puny. And that's one measure of its greatness."

All the ingredients of ambivalence toward Lawrence can be traced to his youth. Anticipating Freud, Alexis de Tocqueville wrote, "The entire man is, so to speak, to be seen in the cradle of the child." Or as the Irish poet George Russell wrote hauntingly:

> In ancient shadows and twilights
> Where childhood has strayed

> The world's great sorrows were born
> And its heroes were made
> In the lost boyhood of Judas
> Christ was betrayed.

T. E. Lawrence was born in Wales in August 1888, but moved to north Oxford with his parents and three brothers when he was eight. His parents, Thomas and Sarah Lawrence, were very different in age, temperament, and social standing. His father was an Irish baronet, his mother a Scottish nursemaid, and their personalities were discordant. More significantly, Lawrence was the name of neither of them and they were not married, so all the boys were illegitimate. But this dark secret was not only covered, it was compensated for by a deep but stern Christian faith that inspired both parents and animated the life of the family.

The Lawrence family had come to Oxford, in fact, because of the influence of a powerful but kind Anglican rector, Canon Christopher. His long ministry at St. Aldate's had touched the lives of thousands of Oxford students and reached out to the Lawrence family in their need. Canon

Christopher remained the dominant spiritual and intellectual influence on the family until his death, aged ninety-three, just before World War I.

All three of T. E.'s brothers were deeply influenced by Christopher. The first became a medical missionary in China, the second a Christian teacher in India, and the third an eloquent speaker at Christian camps. Lawrence, too, was touched indelibly. Though he was to travel far from his evangelical roots and break explosively from his mother's puritanical control, he was active in his faith until his early twenties, and the imprint of his family's faith marked him always.

Educated at Oxford High School and Jesus College, Oxford, Lawrence was known for his flaxen hair, his brilliant blue eyes, his dreamer's vision—and his fascination with the East. Oxford, "the city of the dreaming spires," had bred a dreaming son. Drawn by the lure of the Arab world and tutored by David Hogarth, an Oxford archeologist and Naval Intelligence officer, Lawrence might well have become a world traveler or gypsy scholar if World War I had not fired the furnace that cast his character and reputation forever. Caught up in

helping the Arab Revolt that helped in the libera-
tion of Jerusalem that helped in the downfall of
the Ottoman Empire that helped in the creation of
the modern Middle East, Lawrence—extravagantly
promoted by American reporter Lowell Thomas—
returned to England a mythic hero, a Prince of
Mecca, and "Lawrence of Arabia."

Lawrence was partly fascinated by Thomas's
show about his life, "The Last Crusade," which was
viewed by more than a million people in London
alone. He returned to the theater night after night
to witness what he had become. Partly, though, he
was horrified by the myth and its demands. He
therefore changed his name by deed poll and dis-
appeared into anonymity in the Royal Air Force
as Aircraftman Ross, a deliberate act of self-
degradation that he called "brain-sleep" and "mind-
suicide." And before the many contradictions could
be unraveled, he was killed in a motorcycle crash
in 1935 that left him forever an enigma unsolved.

Did T. E. Lawrence have his own dark secret—
the result of his childhood struggles with the shame
of illegitimacy, his mother's fierce possessiveness,

and the "rape at Deraa" when he was captured by
the Turks? Arguments will continue, inconclusively.
Was Lawrence a fabulist himself as well as the
product of the fantasies of others? To some extent,
certainly. But when all the dust has settled and the
smoke cleared, one thing is beyond question. T. E.
Lawrence made an original and significant contribution to the rise of the modern Middle East,
including the state of Israel and the Arab world—
and he did so as a dreamer and a visionary whose
imagination was the main spring of his action.

Dreaming sets the stage for Lawrence's *Seven
Pillars of Wisdom*. He told a friend he had "col-
lected a shelf of titanic works, those distinguished
by greatness of spirit, *Karamazov, Zarathustra,* and
Moby Dick. Well, my ambition was to make a
fourth." First written in Paris during the Peace
Conference, from notes written daily on the march,
the book is his heroic account of his part in "an
Arab war waged and led by Arabs for an Arab aim
in Arabia." Almost at once he speaks lyrically of
"the sweep of the open places, the taste of the wide
winds, the sunlight, and the hopes in which we

worked. The morning freshness of the world-to-be intoxicated us. We were wrought up with ideas inexpressible and vaporous, but to be fought for."

These dreams, Lawrence admits, were betrayed. "Youth could win, but had not learned to keep and was pitiably weak against age." He had worked for a new heaven and a new earth; the old men's solution was "a peace to end all peace." But one thing always drove him, he says hundreds of pages later in the closing words of the book, "I had dreamed, at the City School in Oxford, of hustling into form, while I lived, the new Asia which time was inexorably bringing upon us. . . . Fantasies, these will seem, to such as are able to call my beginning an ordinary effort."

Lawrence's most stirring statement on vision is in his introduction to *Seven Pillars of Wisdom*. "All men dream: but not equally. Those who dream by night in the dusty recesses of their minds wake in the day to find it was vanity: but the dreamers of the day are dangerous men, for they may act their dreams with open eyes, to make it possible. This I did."

It is a long way from the Oxford City High

School to Aquaba and Wadi Rumm. But is the distance farther or it is in fact closer from a dreaming teenage schoolboy to a thirty-year-old colonel acting his dreams for the Arabs of "an inspired dream-palace of their national thoughts"? Dreamers of the day respond to the gap between vision and reality by closing it.

It would be fanciful to link Lawrence's vision too closely to a Christian understanding of vision, although the schoolboy dreaming he cites exactly coincides with the period of his most ardent faith. But Lawrence's term, "dreamers of the day," is an apt description of answering the call, and it illustrates another highly distinctive feature of calling: *Calling, by breaking through with an outside perspective on the present, is a prime source of Christian vision and Christian visionaries.*

WITH FIRE IN THEIR HEARTS AND WINGS ON THEIR FEET

In practical-minded circles today, it is fashionable to disdain "the vision thing." It is dismissed as idle, dangerous, or a passing phase of life. Certainly vision is a springtime feature of youth, a natural product of energy, idealism, and frustration with the ways things are. The journalist Malcolm Muggeridge, for example, was a convert to faith late in life and celebrated for his irreverent, if not cynical, debunking of pretension and pomposity. But as a young man he was different.

Just after his college days at Cambridge, Muggeridge wrote his own epitaph to a friend: "Here lieth one whose soul sometimes burned with great longings. To whom sometimes the curtain of the Infinite was opened just a little, but who lacked the guts to make any use of it."

Others, however, have made lasting use of vision and imagination—not only in youth but also as a wellspring of life itself. Benjamin Disraeli's climb to eminence as a nineteenth-century statesman was both swift and unlikely. But a clue to the secret of his success can be traced to an early diary entry: "The utilitarians in Politics are like the utilitarians in Religion. Both omit imagination in the systems, and Imagination governs Mankind."

What was true of Disraeli is true too of his whole

people. H. L. Mencken wrote in an essay, "Jews, from time immemorial, have been the chief dreamers of the human race, and beyond all comparison its greatest poets." So as with calling itself, the visionary faith that calling inspires in followers of Christ goes back to the experience of the people of Abraham, Isaac, Jacob, and Moses. There is no god but God and no rest for anyone who has any god but God. God is on the move. Faith therefore means restlessness. The Caller may be unseen and the destination unknown, but those who follow his call have a voice above and vision ahead that subverts every status quo and unsettles every resting place.

Indeed, vision is so central to calling and so explosive in its consequences that it is wise to set it out in direct contrast to the counterfeits that give it a bad name. More particularly, calling's vision must be guarded at three main points. First, we must beware of spurious visions. God's calling inspires and guarantees only those visions that are truly the result of calling. For on the one hand, as the Bible warns, the momentous faculty of imagination has fallen and become the chief human means to aspire to godhead. In the words of the King James translation of the story of the tower of Babel, "And now nothing will be restrained from them which they have imagined to do." But power was not the builders' problem. Their fallen imagination—aided by technology and a universal language—enticed them to reach beyond the limits of the human condition and seek to rival God. After all, Marx, Hitler, and Mao Tse Tung were dreamers too.

On the other hand, vision and imagination, cut loose from the anchor of God's calling, are vulnerable to debunking. Freud distinguished fantasy and daydreaming from artistic creativity and dismissed the former as the product of unsatisfied wishes: "Every single phantasy is the fulfillment of a wish, a correction of an unsatisfying reality." Daydreaming, he says, "hovers, as it were, between three times." Examine it closely and you see that unfulfilled hopes string together past, present, and future "on the thread of the wish that runs through them." Look into a person's fantasies of winning the lottery or lazing on a Tahitian beach and you see what that person thinks of his or her present life.

In short, it is easy to abuse vision and make it serve as chaplain to our conceits or bellhop to our desires. Christian vision, by contrast, must be held accountable because it is inspired directly or indirectly by the call of God. It is an act of imaginative seeing that combines the insight of faith, which goes to the heart of things below the surface, and the foresight of faith, which soars beyond the present with the power of a possible future. This combining of the not-yet-combined is the secret of visionary faith. Vision and reality, word and fulfillment, present and future, situation and possibility, restlessness and reaching out, anger at what is wrong and an aim for what is better—whatever the contrast between the pairs, visionary faith is out to close the gap. This is what makes Lawrence's "dreamers of the day" different from daydreamers— and it is also why they are dangerous: "They act their dreams with open eyes."

Hebrews 11 is the great honors list of visionary faith, a stirring catalogue of men and women whose vision of God called them to live and work against the customs, values, and priorities of their generation. They marched to a different drummer. Their sights were on a different goal. Their home was in a different country. They looked forward to a different city. By their faith they called the entire world into question, and the author of Hebrews says of them, "Those who use such language show plainly that they are looking for a country of their own."

The secret of visionary faith lies in that sentence. How did they manage to transcend their times, surmounting the immediate, living against the generally accepted, looking for the possible beyond the impossible? Called by God, their whole lives were speaking and acting with the language and logic of the alternative vision that is proper to faith. These are the sort of people of whom the newly elected Pope says in Morris West's *The Shoes of the Fisherman*, "Find me men with fire in their hearts and wings on their feet."

Second, we must guard visionary faith by watching out for the pitfalls toward which genuine vision pulls us. Calling-born vision means that followers of Christ do not easily fit into the camps most people join—for example, conservatives and progressives or radicals—yet the fact that we are children of our age means that powerful currents pull us toward one shoal or another.

An obvious example is the difference between the traditional and modern worlds and their tendency to exploit calling in opposite directions. The traditional world had a natural bias toward conservatism and, both then and later, calling was often mistakenly used to justify the status quo. In his *Treatise of the Callings,* William Perkins lays down the rule: "For ever as the soldier in the field must not change his place wherein he is placed by the general, but must abide by it to the venturing of his life, so must the Christian continue and abide in his calling without change or alteration." Like many at the time, Perkins based this advice on Paul's instructions in 1 Corinthians 7, "Abide in your callings"—not realizing that calling is not the word in the original; it had been mistranslated by Luther.

John Calvin had guarded against such a static understanding. "It might seem," he wrote commenting on the same passage, "as though the words conveyed this idea, that everyone is bound to his calling, so that he must not abandon it. Now it were a very hard thing if a tailor were not at liberty to leave another trade, or if a merchant were not at liberty to betake himself to farming. I answer, that this is not what the Apostle intends." What Paul is condemning is "that restlessness, which prevents an individual remaining in his condition with a peaceable mind."

Yet in spite of Calvin, calling was misused to justify the status quo in both the English and the American Civil Wars. In the seventeenth century John Cheke of Cambridge used it to attack the Parliamentary side. Search the Scriptures, he wrote to Oliver Cromwell's supporters, and "we learn not only to fear [God] truthfully, but also to obey our King faithfully and to serve in our own vocation." Worse still, in the United States in 1863 a Southerner attributed the loyalty of four hundred slaves on a North Carolina plantation to regular biblical instruction, including the teaching of 1 Corinthians 7. A Richmond paper of the same period declared, "May we not hope and pray that large numbers [of slaves] will be savingly converted to Christ, thus becoming better earthly servants while they wear with meekness the yoke of their master in heaven?"

In the modern world, by contrast, we have such a bias toward change and progress that this heavy-handed abuse of calling on behalf of conservatism appears ludicrous. But that is because our temptation is the progressive bias, not the static. We insist on choice, we expect change, we prize relevance, we are unthinking believers in the-newer-the-truer, the-latest-is-greatest, and what's in and what's out. We instinctively admire sentiments like George Bernard Shaw's, quoted by Robert F. Kennedy: "You see things as they are and ask 'Why?' But I dream things that never were and ask 'Why not?'" But we are then led by such biases to our own extremes. Since the cultural revolution of the 1960s, "Why not?" has served far more than dreams of justice; it has become the magic word with which to challenge restraint and defy prohibitions. "Why not?" and "So what?" we ask. "It is forbidden to forbid"—"Everything is permitted" in our Lotus-land of freedom. The result of our casual nihilism is a careless demolition of tradition and the creation of a spiritual, moral, and aesthetic wasteland in its place—not only in society but also in the church. Our challenge is not just to see the mistakes of a previous generation, obvious because not ours, but to see as well the problems of our own time, far closer and therefore harder to see.

Third, we must guard visionary faith by watching out for deceptive look-alikes. One modern example is the powerful stream of "self-help" and "positive thinking." With sources far wider than the church, "possibility thinking" has different expressions such as Ralph Waldo Emerson's transcendentalism, Mary Baker Eddy's Christian Science, and William James's "religion of healthy-mindedness." And its popular Christian expressions commonly topple into heresy. Calling, instead of being an objective standard by which we are led, becomes a power to harness for the sake of gaining our own power—and thus the key to health, wealth, popularity, significance, and peace of mind. The result is heresy: Faith in God becomes faith in faith—for our own interests.

An older and deeper look-alike grows from the confusion of visionary faith with the ideal of chivalry. As with positive thinking, the overlap of calling and questing is important—for example, in Francis of Assisi's "troubadours for Christ" and Sören Kierkegaard's "knight of faith." But the timeless appeal of the warrior spirit also has its perils. Above all it serves to justify anything and everything through its ideal of soaring aspirations—including militarism, crusading, cults of violence, male chauvinism, the idolatry of love, or just plain empty-headed romanticism and posturing.

The martial ideal and the strenuous life are appealing to a generation feeling guilty about its comforts and worried about the effects of "over-civilization." But their ideals, their initiations, their testings, their brotherhoods, and their calls to sacrifice are often a counterfeit of the call of Jesus and a dangerous bypath for the pilgrim. As St. Francis cried out to a young knight offering to join him: "Long enough hast thou borne the belt, the sword, and the spurs! The time has now come for you to change the belt for a rope, the sword for the Cross of Jesus Christ, the spurs for the dust and dirt of the road! Follow me and I will make you a knight in the army of Christ!"

The most seductive look-alike today is the ideal of Faustian striving. Adam and Eve, Prometheus, Pandora, Icarus, Johann Faust, Frankenstein—follow the stories through history and literature and the warning is powerful for all to see. Those who transgress boundaries in their all-consuming life search for knowledge, riches, power, and sexual prowess will overreach themselves until their pact with the devil destroys them.

But we moderns have changed the script. Just as in Goethe's version Faust is not damned but saved through his pact with the devil, so we pretend that striving has no limits and no sting. Call it ambition, call it enterprise, call it the competitive spirit, call it the pursuit of excellence, call it the full expansion of human potentialities, call it the will to power—Faustian man bestrides the stage of modern life

with a rage to transgress. Applauded and un-
challenged, he leaps over barriers, flouts conven-
tions, disarms moral judgments, and disdains
prohibitions—blind to his own excesses, and obliv-
ous to his fate.

In our modern giantism of the unbounded ego,
what the Puritans called "Adam's disease" has
become the modern condition. Nietzsche has promoted this spirit most brilliantly:

No one can construct for you the bridge upon
which precisely you must cross the stream of life,
no one but you yourself alone. There are, to be
sure, countless paths and bridges and demi-gods
which would bear you through this stream; but
only at the cost of yourself: You would put yourself in pawn and lose yourself. There exists in the
world a single path along which no one can go
except you: Whither does it lead? Do not ask, go
along it. Who was it who said: 'A man never rises
higher than when he does not know whither his
path can still lead him'?

Who was it? Ironically, perhaps unbeknown to Nietzsche, the original speaker was Oliver Cromwell. In other words, the context was Christian and the theme Cromwell discusses is the truth that makes such striving both possible and yet modest—calling.

Put the claim back on its proper foundations and it is no longer dangerous. "A man never rises higher than when he does not know whither his path can still lead him"—so long as the one who calls him is God. As the writer of Hebrews says, "By faith, Abraham, when called to go to a place he would later receive as an inheritance, obeyed and went, even though he did not know where he was going."

"Every man is made to reach out beyond his grasp," Oswald Chambers writes. Or as he says about himself to his wife, "Hourly almost my sense of His call grows. It will have to be a rover life I am afraid, all over the world. There are grand days coming for you and me." Or again, "Oh what a grand strenuous life there lies out in front of us. The unbribed soul for His enterprises, that is my charge." Dreamers of the day come into their own and stay on course when they follow the calling of Christ.

❧

This brings us to the end of this little book, but only to the barest beginning of the notion of calling and what it means to enjoy a lifetime of answering the call of Jesus. For answering the call of Jesus is the greatest adventure, the deepest romance, and the most fascinating journey of our lives. In embracing the call as your master theme, you will be free. In following it, you will be a leader. In giving up everything for this one way, you will find yourself fulfilled in every way—until one day when the "last call" will sound and you will see the Caller face to face and find yourself at home and free.

LISTEN TO JESUS OF NAZARETH;
ANSWER HIS CALL.

Also Available from Os Guinness

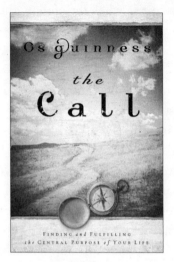

READ THE CLASSIC WORK THAT INSPIRED
Rising to the Call

From the pen of Os Guinness comes a classic reflective work on life's purpose. Far bigger than our jobs and accomplishments and higher than our wildest ideas of self-fulfillment, our calling does more than give purpose and meaning to our lives—it completes God's plan for us.

W PUBLISHING GROUP™

www.wpublishinggroup.com